HOW ARE WE COMPLETE IN CHRIST?

HOW ARE WE COMPLETE IN CHRIST?

But Christ is all, and in all.—COLOSSIANS 3:11.

REV. WILLIAM WHITAKER
FELLOW OF EMMANUEL COLLEGE, CAMBRIDGE

CURIOSMITH

MINNEAPOLIS

Published by Curiosmith.
Minneapolis, Minnesota.
Internet: curiosmith.com.

Previously published as part of *The Morning-Exercise at Cripple-gate, or Several Cases of Conscience Practically Resolved by Sundry Ministers.* London: T. Milbourn, Joshua Johnson, 1661.

The text for this edition is: *The Morning Exercises at Cripplegate, St. Giles in the Fields and Southwark; etc.,* Vol. 1, James Nichols, edit., London: Thomas Tegg, 1844.

The biography is from: Samuel Dunn. *Memoirs of the Seventy-Five Eminent Divines Whose Discourses Form the Morning Exercises Cripplegate, St. Giles in the Fields, and in Southwark.* London: John Snow, 1844.

Unless otherwise stated, the notes and quotes in the footnotes are the original Greek and Latin notes translated into English by James Nichols (1785–1861). When a translation exists, Latin and Greek phrases are sometimes omitted for ease of reading.

Elizabethan verbs and pronouns are updated to modern English word for word.

The "Guide to the Contents" was added to this edition by the publisher.

ISBN 9781946145451

GUIDE TO THE CONTENTS

Biographical Sketch of

REV. WILLIAM WHITAKER, A.M.

his worthy minister was the son of the Rev. Jeremiah Whitaker, one of the most influential divines in the Westminster Assembly; he was an excellent preacher, a universal scholar, an acute disputant, a profound theologian, and a man of unbounded liberality. William was born at Oakham, in Rutlandshire, in 1629. In the fifteenth year of his age, he was admitted to Emmanuel College, Cambridge, where his first tutor gave him this direction, which he constantly observed—"To note every day what, and how much he studied, that in after times, reflecting on his life past, he might repent of the time he had lost." Dr. Holdsworth, who was then master of the college, took such notice of him while a *freshman*, that he gave him the keys of the college library, and appointed him a task in translating Eustatius upon Homer, which he performed, much to his tutor's satisfaction. Here he became particularly noted for his great skill in the oriental languages, which occasioned his being appointed to direct the studies of the junior members of his college. So eminent was he for piety, learning, sweetness of disposition, candour, and ingenuity, that he was beloved and honored of all who knew him.

In the twenty-fourth year of his age, he entered on the ministry, and not only preached peace, but was a peacemaker wherever he came. At Hornchurch, where he was some time a minister, he terminated a controversy of many years' standing, which had cost the parties above a thousand pounds. Dr. Annesley, who preached his funeral sermon, on Zechariah 1:5, 6, says, "That when he preached his farewell sermon to his people in the country, from whom he was torn away by the determination of ministers in the City, there was not only a flood of tears, but the lamentations of many were so loud, that his own voice could scarcely be heard." In 1654, he succeeded his father in the living of St. Mary Magdalen, Bermondsey, and was one of the London ministers, who drew up, and presented to the King, the memorial against the operation of the Act of Uniformity. After his ejectment, he gathered a private congregation, which assembled in a small meeting-house in Long-walk, Bermondsey, where he preached to them as the time would allow, till his death, in 1672. His house, for many years, was full of candidates in divinity, and he had many foreign divines under his care. After his death, eighteen sermons, which had been taken in short-hand, were published by his widow, who prefixed a dedication to Elizabeth, countess of Exeter. Dr. Jacomb added the following account of the author's character: "He was a man of a most sweet and obliging disposition, of an ingenuous temper, and of a courteous and affable deportment. As a scholar, he was richly accomplished in the several parts of useful literature. He possessed great skill in the learned languages, and was well versed in philosophy, philology, and other sciences; but his favorite study was divinity, and to this he directed his principal attention. His natural abilities were very good; and he greatly improved them by study and industry. But he was not one who loved to make a noise or parade of his learning. All his endowments were consecrated to the service of religion, and his character as a Christian. He was a truly pious, sincere, and upright person. He possessed a remarkable tenderness of conscience, and made it his daily exercise to keep a conscience void of offense towards God and man. His life was holy and blameless, becoming one who lived constantly in the fear of God. Humility was a grace that shone in him with distinguished luster. He always thought and spoke meanly of himself, but highly of others; even of many who were much his inferiors. In the character of a minister few excelled him. He was a sound, solid, profitable preacher; and faithful in discharging all the duties of the pastoral office. He was no loiterer in the vineyard; but a diligent and faithful laborer in the work of his great Lord and Master. He sought not his own comfort and ease, so much as the good of others; and few persons were more above the temptations of vain glory and filthy lucre, than he was. In his preaching he was no trifler; he aimed not so much at politeness of language, as solidity of matter; such as might reach the conscience, rather than please the fancy. As he was sound and steadfast in the faith, so his conversation was without stain or blemish. There was an excellent harmony between his doctrine and his practice; as he taught others, so he lived himself. His tenderness towards weak and dejected Christians; his prudence in advising and ordering his ministerial concerns; his admirable union of the wisdom of the serpent with the innocency of the dove; his meekness and patience in bearing wrongs and unkindnesses; together with many other excellent properties of his character—justly entitled him to the veneration and esteem of all true Christians. In a relative capacity, he was an eminent example of filial piety, of conjugal affection, and of faithful friendship. As he succeeded his father in the place of his ministry, so he did also in the possession of his graces; and he preserved to the last, that pious tincture which he had at first received in his education. One cannot but lament, that so excellent a person should have been taken away in the midst of his days. He has two sermons in the Morning Exercises:—How are we complete in Christ?—The Mediator of the Covenant described in his Person, Nature, and Office.

How Are We Complete in Christ?

by Rev. William Whitaker, A.M.

But Christ is all, and in all.—Colossians 3:11.

The great concernment of lost creatures is, above all things, to mind salvation. This is "the one thing needful;" this should be the great *inquiry;*[1] and in the neglect of this, all our other endeavors are no better than laborious trifles. The great danger which even *they* are in *who* seriously mind salvation, is, lest they build upon some sandy foundation, seeking heaven in those ways which lead not thither. The great design of Satan is, either to detain poor undone creatures in a total neglect of salvation, or to deceive them in the way and means thereof. It is therefore the great care of the apostle, as in other Scriptures, so in this, not only to undeceive the world as to those mistakes which prevailed then, but to point out the right, the proper, the only sure, way of salvation; namely,

1 Luke 10:42; Acts 16:30.

through Christ, whom he here declares to be so complete a Saviour, that, as we have "none other,"[1] so we need none other, because "Christ is all."

In the former part of the verse, the apostle shows the insufficiency of all things on this side Christ, to commend us unto God, or stand us in stead in the matter of salvation; and this he does by removing four mistakes at that time common:—

1. *The mistake of the Jews;* who prided themselves in a genealogical kind of sanctity, as being the seed of Abraham. This they account so great a matter, that they cannot be persuaded it could go otherwise than well with them. Let the messengers of God tell them their sins, warn them of their dangers; yet they shelter themselves under this privilege, as that which would be a sufficient bulwark against all kind of threats and comminations; and though John the Baptist in his time,[2] our Saviour in his time,[3] and the apostles in theirs, do all concur in taking them off from leaning upon this broken reed; yet will they not be beaten out of these strongholds. Time was, indeed, when "salvation was of the Jews;" but, that wall of partition being now taken down, and the pale of the church so far enlarged as to take in both Jew and Gentile,[4] no national

---

1 Acts 4:12.
2 Matthew 3:9.
3 John 8:39, 44.
4 Acts 10:34, 35.

privilege can now commend us unto God; nor can a succession of Abraham "according to the flesh" avail us, unless we succeed him in his faith.

2. *The mistake of the circumcised*, whether Jews or proselytes; who, because they had this badge of religion upon them, concluded themselves in a priority for heaven, before all the world besides. But however time was when circumcision was an ordinance of that necessity, that the Lord threatens to punish the neglect thereof, by cutting off that soul from among his people;[1] yet was it not the *outward* but *spiritual* part God accounted of. The apostle, in excluding this, excludes all outward religious observations;[2] as Davenant *in loc.*[3]

3. *The mistake of the Grecians;* who were at that time the masters of all learning; and all other nations, in contradistinction unto them, were styled Barbarians; and of all Barbarians, the Scythians were esteemed the rudest. But whatever worth and excellency may be in human accomplishments; yet all these, in the business of salvation, are but poor matters. It is neither the having nor wanting of these that can considerably advantage or prejudice us in that high concernment.

---

1 Genesis 17:14.

2 Romans 2:29.

3 "In the Jewish religion, circumcision was the principal rite; and is therefore used to designate the observance of all the rites of the law of Moses."—DAVENANT. *(Nichols' trans.)*

4. *The common mistake of the world;* who from their rank and quality in the world are ready to promise themselves a more easy acceptance with God.[1] But "God is no respecter of persons;"[2] he looks upon the children of men with another kind of eye than man is used to do.[3] Whether our outward condition be high or mean, there is nothing of privilege or disadvantage from hence, in respect of salvation.

And as, in the former clause of the verse, the apostle shows the insufficiency of all things beside Christ; so in this clause he shows the single sufficiency of Christ alone. Whatever the Jews promised themselves from their stock and lineage, the proselytes from their circumcision, the Grecians from their wisdom and learning, the great ones of the world from their outward pre-eminencies;—all that, yea, and much more, is Christ to believers. "Christ is all."

This single sufficiency of Christ the apostle proves by a double argument:—

1. *The completeness and perfection of Christ as a Saviour.*—"He is all." Take salvation from first to last, in all the several parts of it, he is the Alpha and Omega, the beginner and perfecter, the author and finisher, of all.[4]

---

1 1 Corinthians 1:26, 27.
2 Acts 10:34.
3 1 Samuel 16:7.
4 Hebrews 12:2.

2. *The way and means whereby Christ imparts and communicates this salvation.*—It is by being "in all." Some read the words as an amplification of the fullness and completeness of Christ: "Christ is all," and that in all things that concern either our present comfort or eternal happiness.[1] Others refer these words, "in all," to those divers sorts of persons spoke of in the former part of this verse; to whom, that Christ may be a Saviour, he disdains not to take up his dwelling in their souls, though lying under all the disadvantages which were then accounted prejudicial. And thus the apostle seems to explain himself, Galatians 3:28, a parallel Scripture unto this. And according to this exposition, as the benefit of Christ's sufficiency is extended to all believers by virtue of their union unto him,[2] so is it restrained and locked up from all unbelievers.[3]

---

1 "Either in all things, or in those intimately connected with our life, or in all of us."—OECUMENIUS. *(Nichols' trans.)*

2 *"In all:* that is, in all believers, who are thus sanctified, and joined to Christ."—DAVENANT *in loc. (Nichols' trans.)*

3 "That *the law is good,* is a result in which we have had no concern; but that *we are wicked in our lives,* is a matter in which we are personally concerned. And it will in no respect prove advantageous to us that the law is good, if our life and conversation be not also good. For the goodness of the law appertains to the office of Christ; but a wicked life has its origin in our own criminality. Nay, we render ourselves the more culpable by our professed attachment to a law which is good, while in our outward observance of it we are manifestly sinful. Indeed, if we be sinners, we are not followers of the

The case to be insisted on from this Scripture is, *How Christians are complete in Christ.*—For the resolving hereof, take this natural deduction from the words:

DOCTRINE

That Christ is a Christian's all.

By "Christian," I mean not them who have nothing more to declare them such than only their baptisms and outward professions; as the church of Sardis.[1] We account them monsters in nature, who have the faces of men, but, in their other limbs, the lineaments and proportions of brute beasts; and how can we account them better than monsters in Christianity, who have the faces of Christians indeed, but withal the hearts and lives of Pagans? That "all which is in Christ, is nothing unto such, except to increase their guilt, and heighten their condemnation. But by the "Christian," I mean him who is αληθως Ισραηλιτης, "an Israelite indeed," as Christ speaks concerning Nathanael:[2] one who labors more to be than seem religious; one whose great care is, that his heart may keep an even pace with his tongue, in all his outward professions.

---

law; because one who really observes the law cannot be called *a wicked observer of it.*"—SALVIAN, *On the Government of God,* book 4. *(Nichols' trans.)*

1 Revelation 3:1.

2 John 1:47.

Now to such Christ is "all." In having an interest in him, they have enough for the supply of all wants, for the prevention of all dangers, for the procuring [of] all good; and therefore, what the apostle speaks here in one word, "Christ is all," he speaks at large, in an enumeration of several weighty particulars: "Who of God is made unto us wisdom, and righteousness, and sanctification, and redemption."[1] We are *foolish* creatures; Christ is "wisdom." We are *guilty;* he is "righteousness." We are *polluted;* he is "sanctification." We are *lost and undone;* but in him is "redemption." We are empty of all good; but he is a full fountain, from whom flow all those blessings which concern either our present comfort or future happiness. We are necessitous and indigent; "in him are hid all the treasures of wisdom and knowledge." Yea, "in him dwelleth all the fulness of the Godhead bodily. And ye are complete in him."[2] Or as you have it in Colossians 1:19, Παν το πληρωμα, "In him dwells all fullness." The rich merchant thought himself no loser by the bargain, in parting with all he had to purchase an interest in Christ.[3] But when never so much is said, there cannot a greater word be used than what the apostle speaks here: "Christ is all." The Greeks were wont of old to account it an excellency to speak much

1 1 Corinthians 1:30.
2 Colossians 2:3, 9, 10.
3 Matthew 13:45, 46.

in few words; to give their auditors, "an ocean of matter in a drop of words."[1] Thus does the apostle here give us, as I may speak, gold in the wedge; which I shall endeavor to beat out into the leaf, by showing how much is comprised in this one word, "ALL." The two names by which the most ancient philosophers were wont to speak of God were, that he was, "the True Being and the Universal Good;"[2] all the scattered excellencies which are dispersed among several ranks of creatures, meeting in him, as the lines of the circumference in the center. This does the apostle speak here of Christ: he is "all." Physicians speak of an universal medicine suited to all diseases, and helpful in all maladies; but whether this can be found in nature or not, yet certainly Christ is a *Panacea;* in him we have a plaster for all sores, a remedy against all distempers. There are indeed thousands of cases wherein all other helps are but "miserable comforters," and physicians of no value; but not one case wherein Christ is not a full and proper help. When all that friends can do is only to pity us, he can help us; because "Christ is all."

For the further explaining and confirming of this great truth, three things shall be spoke to:—

I. *Wherein Christ is all.*

II. *How Christ is all.*

---

1 "πελαγον πραγματων εν σταλαγματι ρηματων."
2 "Το Ον και Το Παν."

III. *What advantage it is to sincere Christians to have their all in Christ.*

I. *Wherein Christ is all.*

In general, he is "all" in all things; for so some of no small account render the following words, "and in all," as has already been hinted. But, more particularly,

1. *Christ is* ALL *to sincere Christians, to free them from whatever might hinder their salvation.*—Salvation is not a mere negative thing, nor does it consist in a bare exemption from hell and wrath, but a translation into heaven and glory. But, alas! betwixt us and glory there is μεγα χασμα, "a great gulf," many bars and impediments. Aye, but Christ is ALL to deliver us from these; and though our deliverance in this world is not complete or perfect, yet is it so far complete as to render our salvation undoubtful, if we be in the number of them to whom Christ is here said to be "all."

The wrath of an offended God, which, like that flaming sword that kept our apostate parents from returning into Paradise, (out of which, because of their apostasy, they had been ejected,) would render our admission into heaven equally impossible. But Christ, by bearing the wrath of God in his own person, has taken it off from ours; and therefore he is said to "deliver us from the wrath to come."[1] He who was the Son of God's love, became the

---

1 1 Thessalonians 1:10.

subject of his displeasure; as appears by comparing Matthew 3:17, with Isaiah 53:10; that we, who were children of wrath, might become the objects of his favor: and, however Christ has not delivered believers from the anger of God as a Father, yet from the anger of God as a Judge. There is an anger that proceeds from love, as the anger of a parent towards that child whose good he desires; and there is a vindictive anger: *the former*, believers are neither freed from, nor would it indeed be their privilege;[1] there is not a greater judgment can befall poor sinful creatures here on earth, than for God not to discover himself angry with them for their sins.[2,3] God then deals with men as a skilful physician with an unruly patient, whom he gives up as desperate; or as a tender parent with a graceless child, whom he utterly rejects. In a word, whatever kind of anger might tend to the prejudice of believers, THAT they are delivered from; but what is for their advantage, THAT they are subject to. That "Christ is all" in delivering from the wrath of God, may further be evidenced by these considerations:—

(1.) *The adequate [cause] of God's wrath is sin.*—There is this difference betwixt wrath and

---

1 Hebrews 12:6–8, etc.
2 Isaiah 1:5.
3 "Great indeed is that wrath which God is treasuring up, while he manifests no tokens of his displeasure against sinners."—HIERONYMUS. *(Nichols' trans.)*

mercy in God: that mercy flows, as I may so speak, naturally from God, and has no other motive but only the gracious and merciful disposition of God. But wrath has always its rise from us; and nothing in us but sin can draw down his wrath upon us. Our meanness cannot, our afflictions cannot: these may sometimes be *the effects* of God's wrath, but never *the causes*. No, it is "because of these things cometh the wrath of God upon the children of disobedience."[1] *Because of these things*, that is, because of these sins, as appears from the verses foregoing. What is it that has filled every age and place of the world with so many dreadful tokens of God's displeasure, but only sin? What was it that cast the angels out of heaven, and degraded them from their first station, but only sin? What was it that drove our first parents out of Paradise, and subjected them, and all their posterity, to so many miseries, but only sin? What was it that brought destruction upon the old world, upon Sodom, Gomorrah, Admah, Zeboim? What was it that broke off the natural branches, and has for so many hundreds of years continued them under a divorce from God, but only sin? In a word, look over all those miseries under which the whole creation groans;[2] and though those miseries in several creatures are divers, yet do they all proceed from the same fountain, namely, sin.

1 Ephesians 5:6.
2 Romans 8:22.

(2.) *Christ is* ALL, *in making expiation for sin.*—He is that "Lamb of God, which taketh away the sin of the world."[1] He is our ἱλασμος and ἱλαστηριον.[2,3] It was not "thousands of rams," nor "ten thousands of rivers of oil," could have borne any proportion in point of satisfaction for our sins. It was not all the legal sacrifices of old could do any thing, nor can all the duties now; but Christ is ALL in expiating for sin.[4] And such is the fullness of Christ's satisfaction, that he has not only freed such as are united unto him from condemnation, but purchased for them the adoption of children.[5] And thus Christ is ALL in removing this bar, and opening this door to salvation, which, had it not been for his mediation, would for ever have remained shut against all the children of men. The pollution and prevalency of corruption, how great an impediment this is to salvation and happiness, was typified by the lepers and unclean persons of old, who were not admitted within the camp.[6] Heaven is no common receptacle for all persons, as Noah's ark was for all sorts of creatures. "Know ye not that the unrighteous shall not inherit the kingdom of God?"[7] *Know ye not?* If you

---

1 John 1:29.
2 1 John 2:2; Romans 3:25.
3 "A propitiation, atonement, or expiation for us."—Nichols.
4 Hebrews 10:5–7, 14.
5 Romans 8:1, 14–16.)
6 Leviticus 13:46.
7 1 Corinthians 6:9.

know any thing in religion, you cannot but know thus much. In the church of God on earth, there is a mixture of corn with chaff, of wheat with tares, of good fish with bad, of sheep with goats; but there shall be a separation of the precious from the vile, and God will come with his "fan in his hand, and throughly purge his floor."[1] Do but consider, and pause a while upon that mischief which sin has done poor creatures by its pollution. How has it stained their glory, cast them down from their excellency, turned angels into devils, and debased man, who was once almost the top of the whole creation, in whom all the scattered excellencies in the book of nature were bound up together in one volume, and met together in a blessed union! How unlike has sin made us to what God at first made us! Those souls of ours, which were once as so many pure beams of light— how is the beauty of them now blotted and darkened! But Christ is that "Fountain opened for sin and for uncleanness;"[2] in his blood is virtue enough to fetch out "scarlet" spots, and "crimson" stains;[3] and if any of the children of men perish in their pollutions, it is not because he wants sufficiency, but because they want faith.[4] Christ is "all" in the business of cleansing and purifying. But, alas! beside the pollution of sin,

---

1 Luke 3:17.
2 Zechariah 13:1.
3 Isaiah 1:18.
4 John 3:16.

there is the prevalency of it. This was to St. Paul so great an affliction, that he who could bear the greatest of outward afflictions patiently,[1] cannot but express something of an holy impatience under this burden;[2] he that could triumph over principalities, powers, life, death, etc.,[3] is yet more than a little discouraged when he reflects upon the corruptions [which] he found lodging in his own heart. Corruption is the great tyrant that has usurped over the whole world; the bounds of its dominion are almost as large as all mankind: there is not a man in all the world, (except the first man Adam, made after God's image, and the Second Adam, who was God as well as man,) but he is born a slave, a vassal to this usurper. The four great successive monarchies, Chaldean, Persian, Grecian, Roman, though the extent of them were great, and the circumference vast, yet were all these limited and bounded: some parts of the world there were which knew nothing of their yoke. But, alas! the empire of corruption reaches every corner of the earth, every person born into the world. We may therefore not unfitly compare it to Nebuchadnezzar's tree, the top whereof reaches heaven, from thence it threw the angels, and the boughs thereof spreading themselves to the ends of the earth;[4] yea, this

---

1 2 Corinthians 11:23, etc.

2 Romans 7:24.

3 Romans 8:38, 39.

4 Daniel 4:11.

vassalage unto corruption, as it is the largest and universalest, so also the miserablest and most dreadful. All other slaveries compared with this, are but like Rehoboam's government compared to his father Solomon's, the least finger of whose dominion, he threatens, should be heavier than his father's loins.[1] We read in Scripture of an Egyptian slavery; in history, of the Spartan slavery, and of the Turkish: all these sad and lamentable; but yet all these reached but the body, and that for a time only; whereas the slavery of corruption reaches the soul, and that for ever, unless Christ become our "Jesus" in saving us from our sins.[2] He has purchased our freedom, and that with a great sum; as the centurion speaks of his Roman freedom.[3] There are none [who] can say with St. Paul, they are born free, except they who are born again, and they are free indeed.[4] Christ is "all" in removing this impediment also, in setting our poor captive souls at liberty from the bonds and fetters of our corruption.[5] It is he alone can conquer these great Goliaths, these untamed affections. But yet even this deliverance is also incomplete in this world; he delivers his people from corruption as to the reign and dominion of it, though not as to the

---

1 1 Kings 12:10.
2 Matthew 1:21.
3 Acts 22:28.
4 John 8:36.
5 Romans 6:6, etc.; 7:25.

presence and disturbance of it: ["That it may not reign; but not yet that it shall not exist."][1]

(3.) *The oppositions of Satan, his wiles and subtilties.*—These are another impediment, and that no small one neither: for if [in] our first parents, in whom there was nothing of ignorance, but a sufficiency of knowledge, there was indeed a nescience of many things, so is there also in the angels;[2] but yet their knowledge was both full and clear in things necessary and pertinent.[3] This was no small advantage against the methods of Satan; because his usual way of mischieving poor creatures has not been so much by force as fraud; not as a lion, but as a serpent; not so much by conquering, as cheating; acting all his enmity under a pretence of friendship, and tempting us to no evil, but under the pretence of some good. The advantage of our first parents was, in this respect, great in respect of their knowledge. Besides, in them was nothing of weakness, but a sufficiency of strength; in them was nothing of corruption, but an universal rectitude and uprightness. The ways by which Satan ordinarily prevails is, either by our ignorance or by our weakness, or else by making a party within us against ourselves. The advantages of our first parents were,

---

1 *Ut non regnet, sed nondum ut non sit.*—NICHOLS' translation is in the text.
2 Matthew 24:36.
3 Colossians 3:10.

in all these respects, far greater than any have against
Satan now; yet Satan prevailed against them. What
cause, therefore, have we to fear![1] But "Christ is all"
to free us from these dangers, to carry us through
these oppositions, who has "led captivity captive,"[2]
who has "spoiled principalities and powers, tri-
umphing over them."[3] But yet, even this deliverance is at present incomplete; for, though Christ has
delivered believers from Satan as a *destroyer*, yet not
from Satan as a *tempter:* he may disquiet such, but
he cannot ruin them.

(4.) *The disturbances and interruptions of a
profane world, its allurements, discouragements,
promises, threats, smiles, frowns.*—Our difficulties
and dangers from hence cannot be little, since the
people of God in all ages have found them so great.
The great advantage which all these outward things
have against us, is their suitableness to our senses; for
though believers are said to "live by faith,"[4] yet the best
of men have had something to witness they were but
men of "like passions," ὁμοιοπαθης, as it was said of
Elias;[5] but "Christ is all" to free us from these dangers:
"Be of good cheer; I have overcome the world."[6] He
has overcome it *for* us, and in some measure in us.

1 2 Corinthians 11:3.
2 Ephesians 4:8.
3 Colossians 2:15.
4 Hebrews 10:38.
5 James 5:17.
6 John 16:33.

2. *Christ is* ALL, *to fill the souls of believers with all that good which may capacitate and qualify them for happiness.*—It is the decree of heaven, that none be admitted into glory but those on whom God has wrought the truth of grace. Heaven must first be brought down into our souls, before our souls are capable of ascending up thither: we must first be "made meet," before we can partake of that "inheritance of the saints in light."[1] We are by nature unmeet, because we are carnal and earthly; and should God dispense with his own decree, and open so wide a door unto heaven and happiness as to let in carnal and sensual persons, heaven would be no heaven unto such; carnal hearts can never relish the sweetness of spiritual enjoyments.[2] Philosophers observe, that all delight arises from a suitableness betwixt the person and the object. What is the reason of that diversity of delights which is among the children of men? That which is one man's joy is another man's grief; and that which is one man's pleasure is another man's pain! The only reason is, because of the diversity of tempers and dispositions. Some there be of such a brutish and swinish temper, that nothing is so pleasing unto them as wallowing in the mire of their sensualities; others, again, of so refined a temper, that they esteem these sensual pleasures very

---

1 Colossians 1:12; Ephesians 5:5.
2 Romans 8:6, 7.

low, and much beneath them. But still every man's delight is according to his temper and disposition; and therefore heaven would be so far from being a heaven unto such, that it would be a kind of hell to them; for as delight arises from an harmony betwixt the person and the object, so all kind of torment, from an unsuitableness and contrariety. Hence is it, that although God vouchsafes us something of heaven here on earth, namely, in his ordinances, yet to unheavenly hearts, every thing of this nature is a *tœdium*, "a burden." "When will the new moon be gone, that we may sell corn? and the Sabbath, that we may set forth wheat?" etc.[1] Ælian reports of one Nicostratus, who, being a skilful artificer, and finding a curious piece of art, was so much taken therewith, that a spectator, beholding him so intent in viewing the workmanship, asked him what pleasure he could take in gazing so long upon such an object; he answers, "Hadst thou my eyes, thou wouldest be as much ravished as I am." So may we say of carnal persons: had they the hearts and dispositions of believers, they would be as much delighted with all means of communion with God as *they* are, and account *that* their privilege *which* now they esteem their vexation. The Greeks tell us, that καλον, "good," is derived απο του καλειν, "from calling," because all good is of an attractive and magnetic nature, to draw forth and call our

---

1 Amos 8:5.

affections after it. But yet it is not the intrinsical excellency of any object that renders it taking with us; but our affections are accordingly exercised upon all kinds of objects, as representations are of those objects from the understanding; for it is the understanding which sits at the stern of the soul, that is the *primum mobile,* "the master-wheel," that puts the affections, as so many lesser wheels, upon motion: therefore, unless our judgments be both enlightened and sanctified, we can never "approve the things that are excellent." Naturalists observe, that, though the loadstone has an attractive virtue to draw iron to it, yet it cannot exercise that virtue upon iron that is rusty. Ignorance is the rust of the soul, that blunts the edge of our affections to whatsoever is spiritually good. There must be, therefore, some kind of suitableness and harmony betwixt our souls and heavenly mercies, before we are capable of tasting the sweetness of them. Now, "Christ is all" to believers in this respect also: it is from "his fullness they receive, and grace for grace."[1] That we have any thing of grace, it is from him; and that we have such a degree or measure of grace, it is from him: "I am come that they might have life, and that they might have it more abundantly."[2] The essence and the abundance are both from him. All those miracles which Christ wrought in the days of his

1 John 1:16.
2 John 10:10.

flesh upon the bodies of poor creatures, in restoring sight to the blind, speech to the dumb, life to the dead—all these does Christ work over again upon the souls of them whom he prepares for heaven.[1]

3. *Christ is* ALL, *to fill all ordinances with power and efficacy.*—These are the means of salvation; and, through his concurrence, effectual means. As they are his institutions, we are under an obligation of using them; and as they have the promise of his presence, we are warranted in our expectations of benefit from them.[2] But yet ordinances are but empty pipes, but dry breasts, unless Christ be pleased to fill them, who "filleth all in all."[3] That there should be such a might and efficacy in things so weak, such miraculous and strange effects by means so inconsiderable; that the foolishness of preaching should be powerful to salvation; it is because it is not man, but God, that speaks: "The hour is coming, and now is, when the dead shall hear the voice of the Son of God: and they that hear shall live."[4] Look upon ordinances in themselves, and so they are τα μη οντα, "things which are not;" but as they are accompanied with the power of Christ, so they "bring to nought things that are."[5] It is he who in baptism baptizes "with the

---

1 Ephesians 5:8; 2:5, 10.
2 Matthew 28:20; 18:20.
3 Ephesians 1:23.
4 John 5:25.
5 1 Corinthians 1:28.

Holy Ghost, and with fire."[1] It is he, in preaching the Word, [who] speaks not only to the ear, but to the heart: "Did not our heart burn within us, while he talked with us by the way, and while he opened to us the Scriptures?"[2] In a word, "Christ is ALL" in every ordinance, in respect of efficacy: while the disciples fished alone, "they caught nothing;" but when Christ is with them, the draught of fishes is so great they are scarce "able to draw it."[3]

4. *Christ is* ALL, *to fill every condition with comfort.*—"The best of conditions is not good without him, nor is the worst bad with him."[4] Alexander accounted himself to live so many days as he obtained victories; but David accounts himself to live more in one day's communion with God, than in a thousand days' enjoyment of all earthly comforts;[5] yea, in the midst of all his earthly confluences, he looks upon all as nothing in comparison of communion with God: "Whom have I in heaven but thee? and there is none upon earth that I desire beside thee."[6, 7] Though he had a kingdom, he values not that. And well might

---

1 Matthew 3:11.
2 Luke 24:32.
3 John 21:3, 6.
4 BERNARDUS.
5 Psalm 84:10.
6 Psalm 73:25.
7 "David does not say, 'There is none upon earth that I have beside thee,' but, 'There is none that I desire, etc.'"
—MUSCULUS *in loc. (Nichols' trans.)*

David be of this mind; for, could we add kingdom to kingdom, and world to world, yet all these, in comparison of the least smile or love-token from God, are no better than nothing; for, "Thy loving-kindness is better than life."[1] The ancient philosophers distinguished betwixt *bona* κατα φυσιν, and *bona* κατα τιμην, "Some things *good in their own nature:*" thus only God: "There is none good but one, that is, God:"[2] "Others *good by way of opinion or estimation;*" and thus all the comforts of this life: whence that maxim of the Stoics: Βιος ὑποληψις, "Life is but opinion and fancy;" and whatever good is in these things is but like those pictures of most deformed and monstrous creatures, which, the poet tells us, had no other beauty than what they owed to the painter's courtesy, namely, the offspring of our own fancies: those who were virtuous were only, by the philosophers, accounted to live; others might *degere*, but not *vivere;* they might "be," but they could not "live." The only true comfort of life consists in living in communion with God. It is his presence [which] fills heaven with all its glory, and it is his presence that fills every condition with all its sweetness. But, alas! how "can two walk together, except they be agreed?"[3] And what agreement can there be betwixt light and darkness,

---

1 Psalm 63:3.
2 Matthew 19:17.
3 Amos 3:3.

the glorious Majesty of heaven and sinful dust, but only through a Mediator? And the only Mediator is Jesus Christ.[1] What was it that enabled the blessed martyrs to account the scorching flames to be beds of roses? What was it that enabled St. Paul to triumph over all kind of adversaries, but only the "love of God in Christ Jesus?"[2] Herein alone consists our comfort, our happiness. Now "Christ is ALL" in this respect also.

5. *Christ is* ALL, *in furnishing us with strength and assistance to persevere.*—The way to heaven is no smooth or easy way, but beset with many difficulties: Τεθλιμμενη ἡ ὁδος·,[3,4] and "we must through much tribulation enter into the kingdom of God."[5] Yea, though the calmness of our passage through this world should be in a perfect serenity from all outward enemies, yet can we not expect a total freedom from the worst of enemies—our own hearts, our corruptions. All the prejudices and mischiefs we either do or can suffer from others, are nothing to what we suffer from ourselves: it is not, *Homo homini lupus,* but, *Homo sibi lupus,* "Men are to none such wolves as to their own souls." Now, inasmuch as the crown of happiness is reserved for

---

1 1 Timothy 2:5.
2 Romans 8:38, 39.
3 Matthew 7:14.
4 "Confined and difficult is the way."—NICHOLS.
5 Acts 14:22.

the head of perseverance;[1] and inasmuch as perseverance in conflicting with such kind of adversaries, (as, though we conquer them yet they are
in us, and though we vanquish them yet still we
carry them about us,) must needs require a greater
strength than our own;[2] it cannot but be esteemed
an eminent privilege to be under the continual supplies of Christ by his Spirit, that after we have put
our hand to God's plough, we may not look back,[3]
and after we have "begun in the Spirit," we may
not end "in the flesh."[4] I speak not this as doubt-
ing the perseverance of them who are sincere, but
as declaring the true foundation on which their
perseverance is bottomed, namely, not any inherent strength [which] they have in themselves, but
those supplies of grace and strength [which] they
continually derive from Christ. There is a vast difference betwixt the best of Christians, considered
singly in themselves, and considered relatively in
respect of their union unto Christ: in themselves, so
weak and impotent that they "can do nothing,"[5, 6]

---

1 Revelation 2:10.
2 Romans 7:24.
3 Luke 9:62.
4 Galatians 3:3.
5 John 15:5.
6 "The Lord says not, 'Without me ye cannot do *much*'; neither, 'Ye will find *great difficulty* in doing any thing'; nor, 'Ye
cannot *perfect* any thing'; but He declares, 'Without me *ye
can do nothing.*'"—AUGUSTINE *in loc. (Nichols' trans.)*

"not sufficient of themselves to think any thing as of themselves,"[1] and yet what can be less than to think? but in Christ mighty and powerful, able to do and bear whatever God would have them: "I can do all things through Christ which strengtheneth me."[2] And thus is Christ the Christian's "all"; thus are they "complete in him."[3]

II. *How Christ is all?*

The resolution of this query is therefore necessary, because many there are who, instead of sucking milk from this doctrine, are ready to suck poison; but, for prevention of all dangerous and unsafe inferences from this great truth, consider,

1. *Negatively*, how Christ is not all.—Not so as to excuse us from all endeavors in the use of means for working out our own salvation. Christ's sufficiency does not excuse but engage our industry; for thus the apostle argues: "Work out your own salvation with fear and trembling. For it is God which worketh in you both to will and to do."[4] As if he had said, "It is God [who] does all; therefore do you what you can."

2. *Positively or affirmatively*, and that in these two respects especially:—

(1.) *Christ is* ALL *by way of impetration*:— Inasmuch as our salvation was his purchase. We may

---

1 2 Corinthians 3:5.

2 Philippians 4:13.

3 Colossians 2:10.

4 Philippians 2:12, 13.

say of our hopes, our helps, our advantages, as the chief priest said of the moneys which Judas had received for the hire of his perfidiousness: "It is the price of blood."[1] Whence is it that they who have brought themselves under the deserts of hell, may have hopes of heaven, enjoy the means of heaven, taste the first-fruits of heaven? All are the price of Christ's blood.[2] It was by his own blood that he entered into heaven himself, and has opened the door to heaven for all that are incorporated into him.[3]

(2.) *Christ is* ALL *by way of application:*— Inasmuch as he brings home the blessings he has purchased unto the souls of his. He has not only purchased salvation for *them,* but them for *it;* not only the possibility of heaven, but a real propriety [proprietorship] in it; and certainly propriety is absolutely necessary unto the refreshment of every comfort. "What are all the treasures of either or both the Indies, to him who only hears of them?" But mere stories. "What all the glories of heaven, to him who is thrust from the enjoyment of them?" But mere torments. There must be a propriety in all spiritual blessings before they can be refreshing; and this alone from Christ. "I give unto them eternal life; and they shall never perish."[4] "I go to

1 Matthew 27:6.
2 Ephesians 5:25–27; Acts 20:28; John 15:13.
3 Hebrews 9:12; 10:19, 20.
4 John 10:28.

prepare a place for you. And if I go and prepare a place for you, I will come again, and receive you unto myself; that where I am, there ye may be also."[1] And what is clearly asserted in these Scriptures, is strongly intimated in those emblems by which Christ is described. What the root is to the tree, the vine to the branches, the head to the body, all this is Christ to believers;[2] namely, not only a treasury of all good, but a fountain continually streaming down all kind of spiritual blessings into their souls; and though faith be both the eye that discerns, and the hand that receives, all from Christ's fullness, yet it is he that by his Spirit works this grace in us. Faith is our *act,* but it is his *gift:* it is we that believe, but it is Christ [that] enables us to believe; so that both in purchasing and applying salvation "Christ is all."[3]

III. *What advantage is it to believers to have their* ALL *in Christ?*

1. *Because our salvation could have been in no hand so safe, so sure, as in the hand of Christ.*— Had it been in our hand by any inherent righteousness, our sad experience [which] we have had of our own unfaithfulness, in sinning away that happiness wherein we were created, may cause us for ever to be jealous of ourselves; but to have it in the hand of Him who is mighty to save, even to the utmost, who

---

1 John 14:2, 3.
2 Colossians 2:7; John 15:1, 5; Ephesians 1:22, 23.
3 Galatians 5:22; Ephesians 2:8; Philippians 1:29.

is so faithful that in all our distresses he is touched with our infirmities; we cannot be so sensible of our own miseries, but Christ is much more;[1] and hence it is that as we have no other Saviour beside him, so is it impossible we should have any like unto him.[2]

2. *Because our salvation could have been in no way so comfortable.*—Because as God has *the glory* of every attribute, so have Christians *the comfort* of every attribute in this way of salvation; for as God has the glory of his justice from them (in their Head and Surety) to whom in this way he shows mercy, "mercy and truth are met together; righteousness and peace have kissed each other."[3] Justice itself, that dreadful attribute to guilty creatures, is in this way of salvation so far from being their enemy, that it becomes their friend, and speaks nothing but what is to their encouragement. And hence it is that sincere believers have, from the very justice of God, answered all manner of discouragements arising from their sins. "Who is he that condemneth? It is Christ that died;"[4] that is, Since God has already received satisfaction from Christ, he cannot in justice require it from the members of Christ, but is just in the "justifying him that believeth in Jesus;"[5] and "if we

---

1 Psalm 89:19; Isaiah 63:1; Hebrews 4:15; 7:25.

2 Acts 4:12.

3 Psalm 85:10.

4 Romans 8:34.

5 Romans 3:26.

confess" and forsake "our sins, he is faithful and just to forgive us our sins, and to cleanse us from all unrighteousness."[1] Thus has the justice of God been their great support in the time of their outward dangers also: "Justice and judgment are the habitation of his throne."[2] In a word, this way of salvation (which was the contrivance of infinite wisdom, and is in itself so mysterious that the angels delight to look into it) does so fully correspond with the condition of poor, weak, sinful, mutable creatures, that it lays a double obligation of praise upon us, that salvation is possible, and that the way of salvation is so complete and full.

The doctrinal part of this observation being thus cleared, one word by way of application.

USES

USE I. *If Christ be* ALL, *then is there no ground of despondency either from your own defectiveness, or the defectiveness of all creature-helps.*—Your duties are defective; your endeavors defective; your very righteousness unsafe to confide in.[3] But though you have nothing in yourselves, yet if you have an interest in Christ, you need nothing more, because in Christ you have ALL.

1. *You have the sum of all.*—Though you have

---

1 Proverbs 28:13; 1 John 1:9.

2 Psalm 89:14.

3 Philippians 3:9.

not estates, friends, worldly comforts; yet in Christ you have what does more than make up the want of all these. We may be as impatiently desirous of this and that earthly comfort, as Rachel was of children, whom we find quarrelling with Jacob, "Give me children, or else I die."[1] But what Elkanah said to Hannah in the like condition, "Am not I better to thee than ten sons?"[2] the same we may say much more to persons interested in Christ: "Is not Christ better to you than all?" The absence of the cistern may well be dispensed with by him who lives at the fountain; and the light of a candle, by him who enjoys the sun. All those seeming contradictions, which so frequently occur in Scripture, can no other ways be reconciled but by the acknowledgment of this. For example: "A father of the fatherless:"[3] how can they be fatherless who have a father? Thus we read of them who were rich in the midst of poverty,[4] who, "having nothing, possessed all things;" joyful in the midst of sorrows;[5] that is, though they had not these comforts, yet they had an interest in Him who is infinitely more and better than all those comforts. Nay, as to inherent righteousness, though you cannot attain a perfection, yet in Christ

1 Genesis 30:1.
2 1 Samuel 1:8.
3 Psalm 68:5.
4 James 2:5.
5 2 Corinthians 6:10.

is perfection. He is ALL.

2. *You have in him the pledge of all.*—According to the apostle's argumentation, "How shall he not with him also freely give us all things?"[1] The inference is strong. Had there been any one mercy that God had thought too great, too much for worthless creatures, it would certainly have been this; but since God has not stuck at giving his Son, this instance of God's bounty is so high that it removes all grounds of questioning his bounty in any thing else. The apostle from this mercy might very well infer a certain subsequence of all other mercies, that might be profitable or beneficial. No ground of despondency, therefore, unto such as are interested in Christ.

USE II. *What cause have we to be thankful for Christ!*—We have cause to be thankful for the meanest of mercies, inasmuch as we are less than the least of all;[2] much more for this which is the highest of mercies. The mercies of our creation, preservation, etc., though never so many and great, are little in comparison of this. It is mentioned as an astonishing act of love, that God should "so love the world, as to give his only Son," etc.;[3] *so* beyond all comparison, *so* beyond all expression. If God has given you his Son, it is more than if he had given

---

1 Romans 8:32.
2 Genesis 32:10.
3 John 3:16.

you a whole world; because it is in him that God has "blessed you with all spiritual blessings in heavenly places."[1]

Use III. *How great is their folly and misery who keep at a distance from Christ!*—Our Saviour mentions it as the highest folly in the Jews, "Ye will not come to me, that ye might have life."[2] There is in Christ the life of justification, to free us from that eternal death to which the law sentences us; the life of sanctification, to free us from that spiritual death under which our apostasy has brought us. There is in him an all-sufficient fullness, for the repairing of all our losses. And are these mercies not worthy the coming for? The apostle puts the very emphasis of the Heathens' misery in this, that they are "without Christ," and therefore without hope.[3] And what is *their misery* shall any of us make *our choice?*

USES OF EXHORTATION

Use I. *Let it be your care that Christ may be* ALL *to you.*—It is no small, nor is it any common, privilege. Many there are who live "without Christ;"[4] others, to whom all that is in Christ is so far from being to their salvation, that it only aggravates their destruction. He that is to some the "chief

---

1 Ephesians 1:3.
2 John 5:40.
3 Ephesians 2:12.
4 Ephesians 2:12.

corner-stone," is to others no better than "a stone of stumbling, and a rock of offence."[1] This was prophesied of Christ: "This child is set for the fall and rising again of many in Israel."[2] There is no mercy so eminently good, but through our corruptions it may become an occasion of evil. Christ himself, the greatest of mercies that ever God vouchsafed to creatures, is yet so far from saving some from their sins, that he only increases their sin. "If I had not come and spoken unto them, they had not had sin: but now they have no cloak for their sin."[3] Those who enjoyed the ministry of Christ in his own person, and were not wrought upon thereby, all their sins would comparatively have been a kind of innocence, had they not discovered such an height of obstinacy. It is therefore no common privilege, "But what should we do that it may be ours?" Take these few directions:—

1. *Labor to get your judgments settled in the belief of this great truth, that all things in the world are a very nothing without Christ.*—That you are poor in the midst of worldly riches, and miserable in the midst of all earthly happiness, while you remain in your estrangements from Christ; and that, of all kind of poverty and misery, this is the worst, because it is in those spiritual blessings wherein consists both our present and future happiness. It is but little those

---

1 1 Peter 2:6, 8.
2 Luke 2:34.
3 John 15:22.

persons understand of their great concernments, that can, with that Gospel "fool," think themselves sufficiently provided for in the things of this world, and say to their souls, as he to his, "Soul, thou hast much goods laid up for many years; take thine ease, eat, drink, and be merry."[1] Do you know you live in this world upon the very brink of eternity? And do you know whether there be more than "one step between" you and another world?[2] And can you take up with any thing on this side Christ? It is an argument [that] you know but little of your own concernments. Some of the grosser Platonists thought the world to be a great animal, and the soul which acted it was God. Now, if the soul be departed from the body, what is it but a mere carcass without life? Christ is the very life and soul of all our comforts; and without him all our creature-enjoyments are but as so many ciphers without a figure, which have no significancy in them, but are so many nothings; nothing in respect of true comfort here, nothing in respect of your preparations for another world. Labor, therefore, through the glass both of Scripture and experience, to behold all the excellences of this world as so many bladders filled with wind, and, at best, to be like Hagar's bottle, which was soon empty,[3] or as broken cisterns. *Cisterns*, and therefore

---

1 Luke 12:19.

2 1 Samuel 20:3.

3 Genesis 21:15.

cannot hold much; *broken cisterns*, and therefore cannot hold what they have long.[1] And withal, let it be your wisdom to look upon Christ as that everlasting Fountain of all good which can never be drawn dry; as that never-failing Spring of all those blessings which will not only sweeten every condition here, but go with us beyond death and the grave. Such fixed apprehensions of these things will be singularly useful to engage our souls in an earnest pursuit after Christ; or, in the Psalmist's words, to "follow hard after him;"[2] and it is his promise, that they that come to him, he will in no wise cast out.[3]

2. *Be speedy in casting out those inmates which, because they are unmeet companions for Christ, may hinder his taking possession of your souls.*— The ark and Dagon could not stand together in the same room; but if the ark stands, Dagon falls.[4] "Can two walk together, except they be agreed?"[5] Christ and our corruptions are at no agreement: these two cannot dwell together under the same roof. If you would have Christ to take up his abode in your hearts, you must prepare a place for him. It was said of David, "He would neither give sleep to his eyes, nor slumber to his eye-lids, till he had found out

---

1 Jeremiah 2:13.
2 Psalm 63:8.
3 John 6:37.
4 1 Samuel 5:4.
5 Amos 3:3.

an habitation for the mighty God of Jacob."[1] The
souls of most men are so crowded with other guests,
that the best entertainment they can afford Christ
is but such as he found in his first entrance into
the world—an out-room, a stable, a manger. But
let it be your care to renounce communion with
all things that might hinder your communion with
him, to "forget thine own people, and thy Father's
house; so shall the king greatly desire thy beauty;"[2]
so, not otherwise; he will have no rivals, no com-
petitors; not a part of our heart, but all.

3. *Be willing to accept of Christ upon his own
terms.*—There can be no terms hard on which we
may gain an interest in him. The great and main
condition is self-denial, together with a full res-
ignation of ourselves to him;[3] and self-denial, if
duly considered, is the greatest self-advantage.
(1.) Because he calls us not to deny ourselves in
any thing that is truly for our spiritual good, or
at least so far as it is for our good. (2.) Though he
calls us to deny ourselves in many outward good
things, yet it is not so much to part with them, as
to exchange them for what is better. (3.) The main
objects of self-denial are those things which it is
our privilege to be freed from; no reason, therefore,
to be offended at such terms as these, to resign up

---

1 Psalm 132:4, 5.
2 Psalm 45:10, 11.
3 Matthew 16:24.

our mistaken judgments to the guidance of Infinite Wisdom, our corrupt wills to his most holy and gracious will, to be in all things at the command of Him whose commands are in nothing grievous, but in all things truth and righteousness.[1] Be therefore as willing to be his, as you are desirous he should be yours: the consent must be mutual, or else the match can never be made up betwixt Christ and your souls.

4. *Measure all things by their reference unto Christ.*—Of all good things, account them the best which may promote your endeavors after that good which is the highest; as ordinances, the means of grace, which at how high a rate they are valued by David, may appear from his pathetical and most affectionate desires of waiting upon God in them.[2] Of all evil things, account them the worst which estrange you from Christ, the truest good; and therefore let your only impatience be of sin, as that which only "separates between you and your God."[3] The observation of this rule will very much secure you from all diversions, and quicken you in your endeavors after an interest in Christ.

USE II. *Be serious in resolving this great question— whether Christ, who is* ALL *to sincere Christians, be* ALL *to you.*—It is a question of that importance,

---

1 1 John 5:3; Psalm 119:151, 172.
2 Psalm 27:4; 42:1, 2; 63:1, 2.
3 Isaiah 59:2.

that all your comfort depends upon the resolution of it, yea, all your hopes. Take these two characters:—

1. *Are you conformable unto Christ.*—Is the same mind in you that was in him?[1] Are you holy, and humble, and self-denying, and in all things followers of that pattern which he has set before you in his own example? "He that is joined unto the Lord is one spirit."[2] "Old things are passed away; behold, all things are become new."[3] Causes are best known by their effects, trees by their fruits, fountains by their streams; so is our interest in Christ by this effect thereof, our conformity unto Christ.

2. *Are you* ALL *to him?*—It is but a just retaliation in Christians to be so, and it is withal an evidence that "Christ is all" to them.

(1.) Are you ALL to him in your *affections*, in prizing him above all? Can you, with the spouse, esteem the love of Christ "better than wine;"[4] with David, "better than life?"[5] Can you, in the midst of all your creature-comforts, account all as nothing in comparison of him? and say, with Asaph, "Whom have I in heaven but thee? and there is none upon earth that I desire beside thee."[6] So high were Moses's affections, that he esteems "the

1 Romans 8:9; Philippians 2:5.
2 1 Corinthians 6:17.
3 2 Corinthians 5:17.
4 Song of Solomon 1:2.
5 Psalm 63:3.
6 Psalm 73:25.

reproach of Christ greater riches than the treasures in Egypt."[1] And, indeed, if Christ be but an underling in our affections, it is an argument we have no part in him. "He that loveth father or mother more than me is not worthy of me: and he that loveth son or daughter more than me is not worthy of me."[2] The affections are the truest pulse of the soul, the most genuine and natural symptoms of its frame and temper. It is these that speak the proper idiom and language of the heart. Make use of this rule therefore—Is Christ uppermost in thy heart? Your affection to him is an evidence of his to thee.

(2.) Are you ALL to him in your *acknowledgments*, in ascribing all to him? Thus St. Paul: "By the grace of God I am what I am."[3] That my condition is not better, it is from myself; that it is so good, it is from him.[4]

(3.) Are you ALL to him in your *contentment and satisfaction*, accounting you have all in him, though you have nothing beside him? "Although the fig-tree shall not blossom, neither shall fruit be in the vines; the labor of the olive shall fail, and the fields shall yield no meat; the flock shall be cut off from the fold, and there shall be no herd in the stalls: yet I will rejoice in the Lord, I will joy in the

---

1 Hebrews 11:26.
2 Matthew 10:37.
3 1 Corinthians 15:10.
4 Ephesians 5:20.

God of my salvation."[1]

(4.) Are you ALL to him in your *dependences and expectations*, in seeking all from him? The highest condition of grace needs further grace; but in Christ are all supplies. It is an argument of our interest in him, when in all distresses we make him our refuge, in all weaknesses our strength.

(5.) Are you ALL to him in your *designs and aims*, in seeking his glory, beyond your private advantages? This was St. Paul's design in life and death, that Christ might be magnified;[2] and if you be thus all to Christ, it is an evidence "Christ is all" to you. And how well are they provided for, who have Him who is all for their portion!

---

1 Habakkuk 3:17, 18.
2 Philippians 1:20.